Bugs, Bees, and other Buzzy Creatures

DK

Senior editor **Wendy Horobin**
US editor **Margaret Parrish**
Editorial assistant **Sophia Danielsson-Waters**
Senior designer **Claire Patané**
Designer **Charlotte Bull**
Design assistants **Eleanor Bates, Rachael Hare**
Photographer **Ruth Jenkinson**
Producer **Leila Green**
Producer, Pre-Production **Andy Hilliard**
Jacket designer **Charlotte Bull**
Jacket coordinator **Francesca Young**
Creative technical support **Sonia Charbonnier**
Managing editor **Penny Smith**
Managing art editor **Gemma Glover**
Art director **Jane Bull**
Publisher **Mary Ling**

First American Edition, 2016
Published in the United States by DK Publishing
345 Hudson Street, New York, New York 10014

Copyright © 2016 Dorling Kindersley Limited
DK, a Division of Penguin Random House LLC
16 17 18 19 20 10 9 8 7 6 5 4 3 2 1
001–285433–April/2016

All rights reserved. Without limiting the rights under the copyright
reserved above, no part of this publication may be reproduced, stored
in or introduced into a retrieval system, or transmitted, in any form, or
by any means [electronic, mechanical, photocopying, recording, or
otherwise], without the prior written permission of the copyright
owner. Published in Great Britain by Dorling Kindersley Limited.

A catalog record for this book is available
from the Library of Congress.
ISBN: 978-1-4654-4477-6

DK books are available at special discounts when purchased in bulk
for sales promotions, premiums, fund-raising, or educational use. For
details, contact: DK Publishing Special Markets, 345 Hudson Street,
New York, New York 10014 SpecialSales@dk.com

Printed in China
All images © Dorling Kindersley Limited
For further information see: www.dkimages.com

A WORLD OF IDEAS:
SEE ALL THERE IS TO KNOW
www.dk.com

Parents

This booked is packed with activities for your little ones to enjoy. We want you all to have a great time, but please be safe and sensible—especially when you're doing anything that might be dangerous (or messy!) Have fun.

Contents

4   Let's count legs

6   Boxy bugs

8   Wriggly caterpillars

10   Butterflies

12   Darting dragonflies

14   Dragonfly clips

16   Hoppers and crickets

18   Buzzy bees

20   Honey cookies

22   Brilliant beetles

24   Lots of spots!

26   Ladybug pebbles

28   Awesome ants

30   Amazing ant maze

Let's count legs

Bugs come in all **shapes** and **sizes**.

You can often tell which **type** you are

looking at by counting its legs.

Six legs

6

If a creature has six legs, say hello to an insect! All insects have six legs. Bees, beetles, and ants are insects.

Eight legs

How many legs does this one have?

8

Can you count eight legs? If so, you are looking at a spider or scorpion. They always have eight legs.

Shake a leg

Insect legs are not just for walking and running. Insects use their legs for jumping, climbing, swimming, digging, holding their food, and making noises.

No legs

Slugs don't have any legs, but they do have a foot.

Worms move by wriggling.

Lots of legs

20+

Centipedes have one pair of legs on each body segment. They can run very fast.

Hundreds of legs

Millipedes have short, stubby legs.

100+

One, two, three, four, five... too many legs to count? That's a millipede. Some have 750 legs!

5

Boxy bugs

You can make **all kinds of bugs** out of an egg carton. Try a **spider** or a **caterpillar**.

You will need:
Egg cartons
Paint
Scissors
Pipe cleaners
Googly eyes

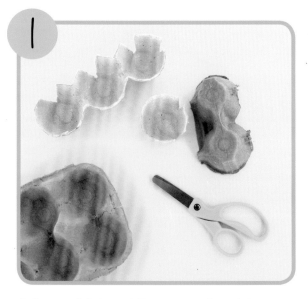

1

Ask an adult to cut the egg cartons into strips. Use one bump for a spider, two or three for a beetle, and a row for a caterpillar.

2

Paint your bug's body. If you like, you can add spots or stripes, or make each of the bumps a different color.

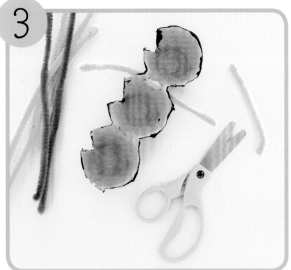

3

Ask an adult to cut pipe cleaners into equal lengths to form legs. Push them between the bumps, then bend the ends up into feet.

4

Twist some pipe cleaners around a pencil to make feelers and poke them into the head. Add eyes and a mouth, and you have a bug!

Wriggly caterpillars

Look closely at a plant and you may see a caterpillar **wriggling** up a stem or **chewing holes** in a leaf. Very soon it will change into something **amazing**.

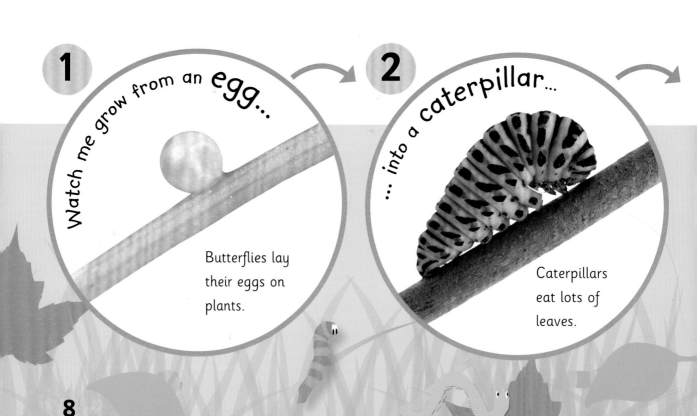

1 Watch me grow from an **egg**...

Butterflies lay their eggs on plants.

2 ...into a **caterpillar**...

Caterpillars eat lots of leaves.

Did you know?

Not all caterpillars become butterflies— some turn into moths.

3

...then a **chrysalis**...

A hard case protects the caterpillar while it is changing.

4

...and, finally, a **butterfly!**

Butterflies

Hang up these **butterflies** so they can **flutter** in the wind.

You will need:
Cardboard tubes
Paints
Colored paper
Scissors
Craft glue and tape
Pipe cleaners
Googly eyes

1

Paint a cardboard tube and let it dry. This will be the body of your butterfly. While it's drying, make the wings.

2

Fold a piece of paper in half. Draw a capital "B" along the fold and cut around it. Open out the wings and decorate with colored paper.

3

Apply a line of glue along the middle of the butterfly's body, then stick the cardboard tube to the wings and let it dry.

4

Twist two pipe cleaners around a pencil to make feelers and stick them on with tape. Add eyes and draw on a friendly smile.

Tape thread to the back of your butterfly so you can hang it up.

Darting dragonflies

See that? It's a **colorful dragonfly** flying over the **water** at **superspeed**. If you blink, you might just miss it!

Water birth

Dragonflies are born in water and live there for several years. This is why adult dragonflies are usually found by ponds, rivers, and lakes.

Dragonflies have long, thin bodies and large heads.

Dragonfly babies are called nymphs.

Did you know?

Dragonflies are the most successful hunters in the insect world and almost always catch their prey.

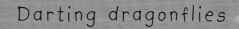

Fast fliers

These amazing acrobats use their two sets of large wings to fly at great speeds, change direction instantly, hover in place, and even fly backward.

Deadly hunters

They may be pretty, but to other insects they're very scary. Dragonflies can eat hundreds of flies and mosquitoes every day.

Dragonflies have huge eyes that allow them to see in many directions at the same time.

13

Dragonfly clips

Use a **dizzy** dragonfly to keep your **bits and pieces** of paper neat and **tidy**.

You will need:

Clothespins
Paints and paintbrush
Colored paper
Scissors
Markers
Craft glue
Googly eyes

1 Paint a wooden clothespin or decorate a colored plastic one. This will be the body of your dragonfly.

2 Fold a piece of colored paper in half and ask an adult to cut a heart shape to make a pair of wings. Decorate with paints or markers.

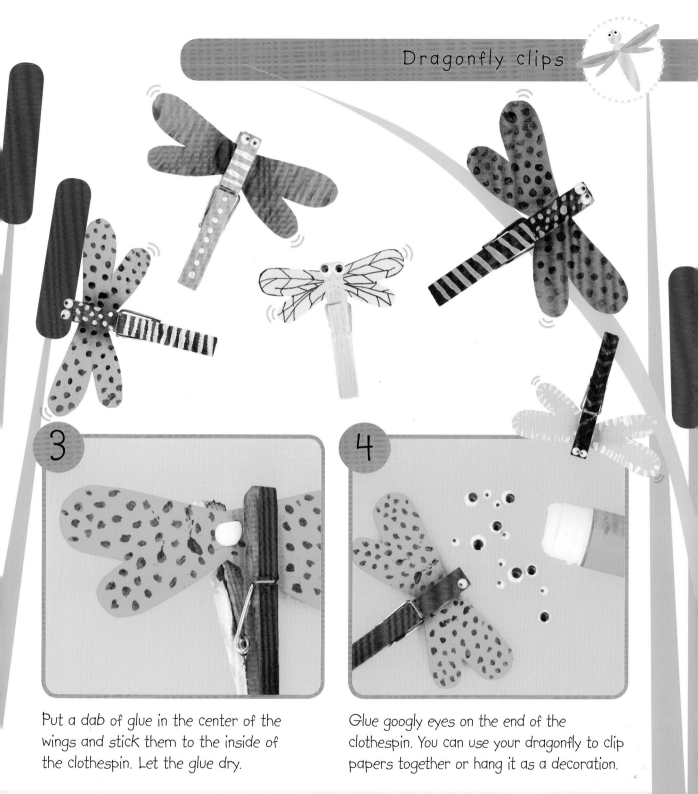

Dragonfly clips

3

Put a dab of glue in the center of the wings and stick them to the inside of the clothespin. Let the glue dry.

4

Glue googly eyes on the end of the clothespin. You can use your dragonfly to clip papers together or hang it as a decoration.

Hoppers and crickets

Grasshoppers and **crickets** are similar bugs that are known for **making noise** and **jumping around!**

Grasshoppers and crickets look similar, but crickets have shorter antennae. This is an easy way to tell them apart.

Did you know?
Crickets "sing," by rubbing their wings together to make a loud noise.

Grasshoppers love the daytime, and crickets mostly come out at night.

Catapulting crickets

Although most crickets and hoppers can fly, they're best known for jumping. Some can jump 10 times their body length!

Grasshoppers make noise, too—but they do it by rubbing their legs against their wings.

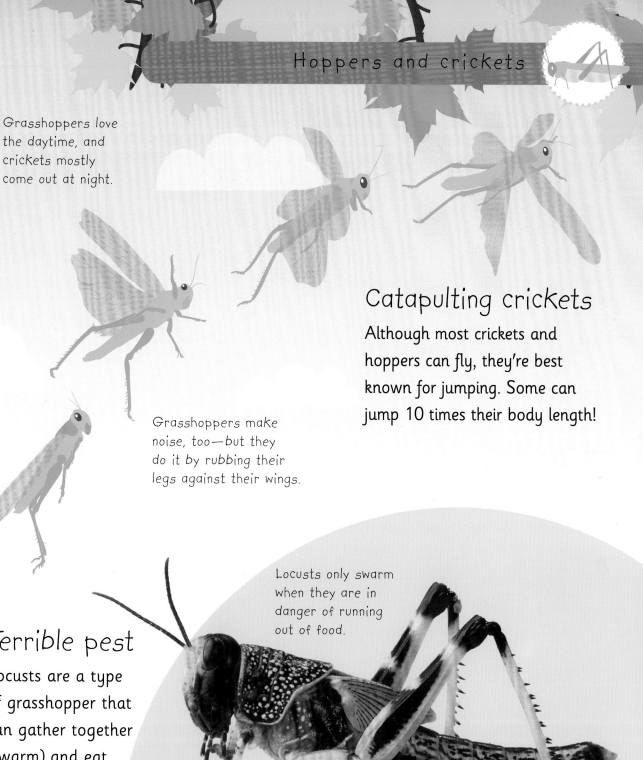

Locusts only swarm when they are in danger of running out of food.

Terrible pest

Locusts are a type of grasshopper that can gather together (swarm) and eat crops, ruining a harvest.

Buzzy bees

Bees are busy insects. Every day they fly off to collect **nectar** from hundreds of flowers, which they turn into sweet, golden honey.

BUZZZZ

Pollen basket

The buzzing noise is made by their wings when they fly.

Bumblebees

These plump, striped bees have long, fuzzy hair all over their bodies. They have baskets on their back legs for collecting pollen.

Did you know?

It takes the nectar of two million flowers to make one jar of honey.

Honeybees

Honeybees live in large groups. Their nest is called a hive.

When a honeybee finds flowers with lots of nectar it does a waggle dance to tell the others where to find them.

Bees build six-sided wax "rooms" to store honey. Eating honey helps them survive through the winter.

BUZZZZ BUZZZZ

Honeybees busy building a honeycomb.

19

Honey cookies

Become a **busy bee** **yourself** by making these **yummy** honey **flower** cookies.

Ingredients

8 tbsp butter
²/₃ cup sugar
1 tbsp honey
1 egg yolk
1 cup all-purpose flour
1 tsp cinnamon

Beat the butter and sugar together in a bowl until they are pale and creamy.

Next, add the honey and egg yolk and mix together.

Sift the flour and cinnamon into the bowl, then mix until everything forms a soft dough.

Sprinkle flour on a board and a rolling pin. Roll out the dough until it is ¼in (5 mm) thick.

Preheat the oven to 350°F (180°C). Cut out flower shapes with a cookie cutter.

Ask an adult to put the sheet in the oven.

Place the cookies on a baking sheet. Bake in the oven for 12–15 minutes, until golden brown.

For the icing

1 cup confectioners' sugar
3 tsp water
Piping bag
Sprinkles

Mix the confectioners' sugar with the water to form a thick paste. Put it into a piping bag and decorate your cookies.

You can add some pretty sprinkles.

Brilliant beetles

You're never far from a **beetle**. Hiding under **leaves**, crawling, swimming, or **flying**, they are almost everywhere!

You can find beetles in lots of colors.

Nearly half of all insects are beetles!

A hard, shiny casing protects beetle's wings.

Little and large

Some beetles are so teeny tiny they could fit on a pinhead. Others are giants, measuring around 8in (20cm) long.

Some beetles destroy trees and crops.

Did you know?

Beetles cannot see very well so they release special smells to communicate.

Did you know that ladybugs are beetles?

Lots of spots!

Ladybugs are **shiny**, round, spotted **beetles** that come in many colors. Let's see how many **spots** these ladybugs have.

...four...

4

Did you know that ladybugs can fly?

Two spots...

2

... six....

6

How many **ladybugs** can you count?

... seven...

Did you Know?

The ladybug's bright colors warn birds that they are not tasty to eat.

7

... nineteen...

19

twenty-nine!...

29

Ladybugs can have a few spots, many spots, or no spots at all. Some of them have stripes instead!

Ladybug pebbles

Create your **own family** of **little** ladybugs. All you need are **pebbles** and paint!

You will need:
Smooth, bug-shaped pebbles
Acrylic paint
Paintbrushes

1

Gather your pebbles and scrub them thoroughly to make sure they're nice and clean. Dry them well.

2

Cover as much of the pebble as you can with black paint. Let it dry. When it's dry, turn it over and paint the other side.

3

Paint oval-shaped wing cases on one side of the pebble. These are usually red, yellow, or orange. Let them dry. Paint black spots.

4

Once the spots have dried, paint a friendly face on the front. Make more ladybugs with different numbers of spots.

Bugs, bees, and buzzy creatures

Awesome ants

Ants are amazing insects. **Millions** of them live and work **together** to look after and **protect** their nest.

Leaf-cutter ants take leaves and flowers back to the nest for food.

Ants use their feelers to touch, taste, and smell.

28

One two, three, four...

When ants find food they leave a scent trail that leads other ants to the food.

Girl power

Most ants are female. They build the nest, protect it against invaders, and collect food for the colony.

Did you know?

There are thought to be one million ants for every human on Earth.

Super ants

Ants are incredibly strong for their size. Some of them can lift objects that are more than 20 times their own weight.

Ants often build their nests underground.

Amazing ant maze

Ants live in large groups called **colonies.** Many colonies have underground nests.

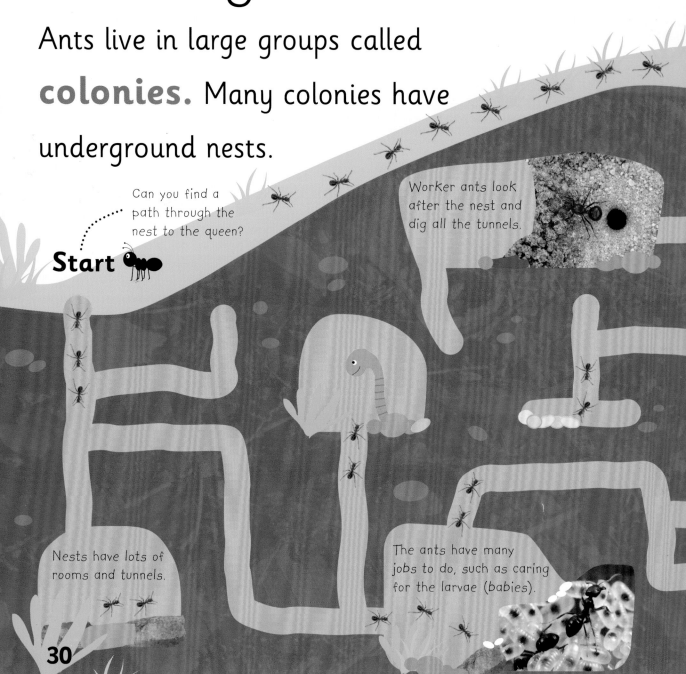

Can you find a path through the nest to the queen?

Start

Worker ants look after the nest and dig all the tunnels.

Nests have lots of rooms and tunnels.

The ants have many jobs to do, such as caring for the larvae (babies).

Help the ant reach the queen

Not all colonies are built underground; some ants build nests in tree trunks.

Food is brought from outside and stored in large rooms.

The queen is the most important ant in the colony. She gets to have the biggest room!

Finish

31

Index

• A •
Ants 4, 28–29, 30–31

• B •
Bees 4, 18–19
Beetles 4, 22–23
Butterflies 8–9, 10–11

• C •
Caterpillars 6, 8–9
Centipedes 5
Clothespins 14–15
Cookies 20–21
Crickets 16–17

• D •
Dragonflies 12–13, 14–15

• E •
Egg cartons 6–7

• G •
Googly eyes 6–7, 10–11, 14–15
Grasshoppers 16–17

• H •
Honey 18–19, 20–21

• L •
Ladybugs 4, 23, 24–25, 26–27

Legs 4–5, 17
Locusts 16–17

• M •
Maze 30–31
Millipedes 5
Moths 9

• P •
Pebbles 26–27
Pipe cleaners 6–7, 10–11

• S •
Scorpions 4
Slugs 5
Spiders 4, 6–7

• W •
Worms 5

Acknowledgments

The publisher would like to thank the following
for their kind permission to reproduce their photographs:

(Key: a-above; b-below/bottom; c-center; f-far; l-left; r -right; t-top)

5 Colin Keates (c) Dorling Kindersley, Courtesy of the Natural History
Museum, London (br). 12 Dreamstime.com: Andersastphoto (bl). 22
Colin Keates (c) Dorling Kindersley, Courtesy of the Natural History
Museum, London (bl). 23 Fotolia: Eric Isselee (tcr); Fotolia: giuliano2022
(bcr); Dreamstime.com: Vladvitek (cr). 28 Dorling Kindersley: Thomas
Marent (bl). 30 naturepl.com: Ann & Steve Toon (cr); Visuals Unlimited
(br). 31 naturepl.com: Steven David Miller (cb).

All other images © Dorling Kindersley
For further information see: www.dkimages.com

Thanks to Lucy Claxton for picture library help, and
James Mitchem for editorial assistance.